Editor
Evan D. Forbes, M.S. Ed.

Editor-in-Chief
Sharon Coan, M.S. Ed.

Illustrator
Barb Lorsedeyi

Cover Artist
Keith Vasconcelles

Art Director
Elayne Roberts

Product Manager
Phil Garcia

Imaging
Alfred Lau

Publishers
Rachelle Cracchiolo, M.S. Ed.
Mary Dupuy Smith, M.S. Ed.

Critical Thinkir

S0-ALI-480

Brain Teasers

Grade 1

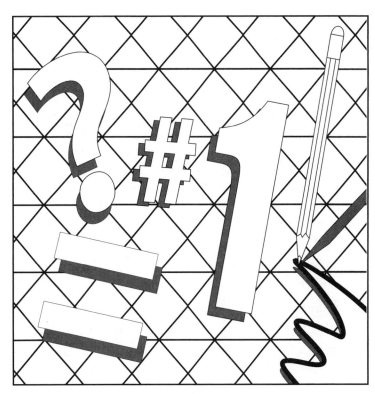

Author
Dona Herweck Rice

Teacher Created Materials, Inc.
6421 Industry Way
Westminster, CA 92683
www.teachercreated.com

©1995 Teacher Created Materials, Inc.
Reprinted, 2001 WESTERN EDUCATIONAL ACTIVITIES LTD.
12006 - 111 Ave. Edmonton, Alberta T5G 0E6
Made in U.S.A. Ph: (780) 413-7055   Fax: (780) 413-7056
ISBN-1-55734-486-8   GST # R105636187

Teacher Created Materials

Table of Contents

Introduction

Brain Teasers provides ways to exercise and develop brain power! Each page stands alone and can be used as a quick and easy filler activity. The pages can be distributed to students as individual worksheets or made into transparencies for presentation to the entire class at once. The book is divided into sections so the teacher can find activities related to a subject being taught or to a particular student's needs. The activities are especially useful in helping students develop:

- logic and other critical thinking skills.

- creative thinking skills.

- visual discernment skills.

- reading skills.

- spelling skills.

- vocabulary skills.

- math skills.

- general knowledge skills.

Name _____

Dot to Dot

Follow the numbers to find the picture. Color the picture.

29 30   33
28   31 32   34
26 27   36
25 24   35 37
38
1 39
4
3 2 40

23

22

21

18   11
10 7
17 14
20
19

16 15 13 12   9 8 6 5

Name _____

Follow the Dots

Follow the even numbers to find the picture. Color the picture.

Name _____

Follow the Letters

Follow the letters of the alphabet to find the picture. Color the picture.

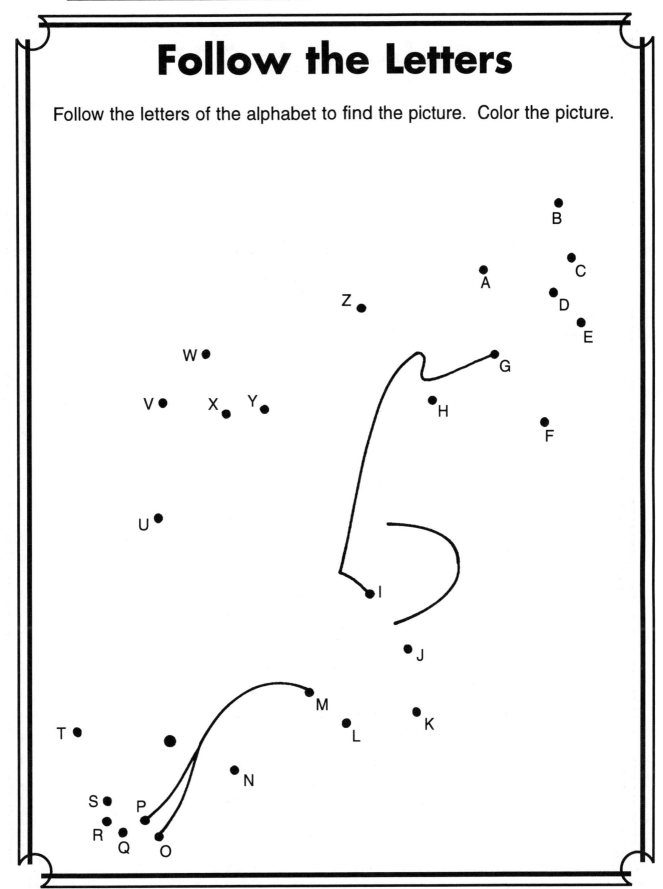

Name _____

Backwards ABC

Follow the letters of the alphabet backwards to find the picture. Color the picture.

6

Name _____

It's Amazing

Follow the maze to get the goldfish to the bowl.

Name _____

A Maze of Letters

Follow the alphabet through the maze to get the children to school.

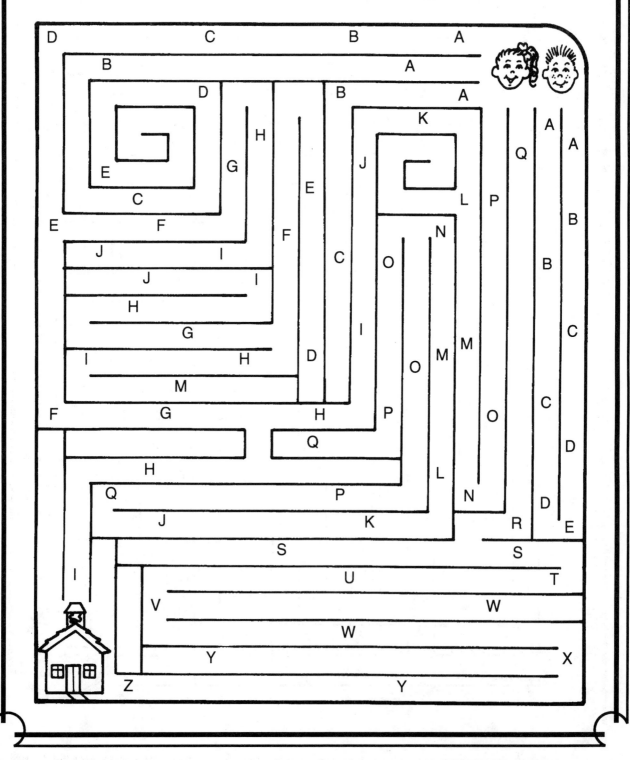

Name _____

Amazing Numbers

Follow the numbers 1 through 20 to get the bear cub to its mother.

Name _____

Body Works

Find all the words from the Word Box in the word search puzzle. The words can be found down or across.

```
L R J T X L V F D G N B L R N J Y B J S D H Y C
M F Q W Q B Y Q X F H T X T H T N K B D S X P F
C M H W T B B S Q S M G D G Q X V R B X F T Q G
L D P R S V C G S Y X Y L S N V P P W M N Z W R
G X V V Q R L T H S D V X X J Y B H G P G D K K
K F C X L Q S V O F P X L B W H D T N L Z X V B
N T C L R Y Z S U N V T C N V L S Q J A R M M C
D S H B K H B X L N P F H R G D F R G N X T R C
Q D M T J A L B D D L G E A M K O M S K T C Y B
X X B G G I L Y E R Z R E H Z T O X L L L R N D
F I N G E R F F R N E C K W W M T O E E L B O W
F H T M R M Y Z M M B T K R Z N Y F Y A G H S G
H B D H K W V R H O X M N W N C V C E R X E E L
Z N L B V N L B N U M K E P D S L B J M F A L C
H E E L H A N D Q T Y G E S T O M A C H Y D X G
B R G K Z C X P X H Z B C L J H J Y L R P Z S S
M S P B C V V F V C P T M C J Z B D J P G D X G
```

Word Box

head	knee	nose	heel
arm	toe	ear	ankle
leg	finger	eye	stomach
foot	shoulder	mouth	cheek
elbow	neck	hand	hair

Name _____

Things That Go

Find all the words from the Word Box in the word search puzzle. The words can be found down or across.

```
S Y B M T R N L Q J P V R Q S T C C C S N B V
H K G F R G F X T T G X C V W C L W W D W D W T
I H G Q I L W L F K F B J W S P C B F P Y K F M
P M M L C L X G F Z Y F S C J S H B S X R L M S
R S F W Y P V G K W Q K D B J X R M B S L D K H
N S B Z C M H Y T M T S B G K J L D Z W Y V K Z
J V Y R L B Z T Q W H M H Y D Y L S C Y J T L B
D M B K E Y J Y G Z G O P D C P V K G V B C K H
T B P V T F C G Y S P T T S L E D S Z L G W B V
R T V X R R T V N S S O B R C Z G C Q S T N J B
P L D B A S K A T E S R C N L L V O W A G O N J
L L X Y I S M G B S K C C X G Z N O J E E P B P
A C A R L D H L O G L Y P K K Z T T Y A G B V V
N H S A E N N A A J S C V C A S L E N X E O A M
E B R T R A I N T R O L L E Y K T R U C K P N D
Z U F P V W G M N E S E P V A H Z N S J C B Y H
Y S U R F B O A R D S M F D K B I C Y C L E J M
```

Word Box

train	car	truck	bus
plane	bicycle	jeep	trolley
van	trailer	boat	kayak
ship	skates	surfboard	scooter
tricycle	wagon	sled	motorcycle

Name _____

I Only Have I's for You

Find the "I" words hidden in the word search puzzle. The words can be found down or across.

```
D D R T L B H M R V H C Q D F H H B Y R M B D R
Y H M X Y S S F T X T W S P T H Z D B Q V V F H
Q L K Q N J J Z X K Y K J P T Q P P G B F Y P Q
D Q H M N N N Z J S Y S K M N Y P J R M W D H R
  I H W F R C X V Z V F J G M V N B Y H Z
G H T Y I H L T Q C W K M V S G W I S P
U I L L C C X R V W W V Q Z V C W G X Y
A K I Z I R J P T B I X M H F Y J L W L
N W S J C M B I Z P C V C I F Q Y O F M
A I D O L C P F I T E M G T Y N R O R C
M F Y P E C T J B S F X K L B B C M M S
B Y N R J T H F P G Z X C Q P S M M Y N
J P Z I J B I W D M B V Q F S K J P T H
B N O N C V T E W X F T U I J K L M B V
P L N T Y B M L P A A S D E W Y U I O P
F J T L B O I R I S W Z Q M L G S C T T W V X W
Q J F G W S F V C G L K B Y S B C P Q Z G K W N
M K R L J Q F M X C R R V Z R G W P X M T J V V
S N H F D M P Y N W W B M H J T Y V C B D P W V
```

Word Box

it	ill	if
item	iguana	into
igloo	iris	is
ice	idol	icicle

Name _____

Lights, Camera, Action!

Find the action words from the Word Box in the word search puzzle.
The words can be found down, across, or diagonally.

```
N R N B S W S P M R N J N L R L B S H K M J R Z
X R N L G V S C P L G W N P A G I U F Q R H J K
S R M X J H B V C N G F D L R U R S I S E Y U V
M L B T L D N Z V A L F H A E U G X T L A G M S
S L O O K F P A I N T C R Y A W N H J E D Q P X
K W Y R V Q S Q P T H C F O T M T R O E N X R M
I B I V L N L N X N R B H C W L Z L G P H C K J
P W R M H Q I D P V O R X O P N T D L S F W V H
C S G E X P D F F K W D H U X J H H D M Z N D F
L J K K A N E R N F B Y N G W F K O H I T Y T Q
I B Q T C K X Y Y D M C Y H X M H W P L Z W S B
M P N M M D Y R X G S L M Q T B X G L E D Y G C
B H W G V D C R V S V C Y G Z Z B Y H T X G S H
T V D W V W C P V W R F N P Y K Y M F T H Y V F
Q J V D R L F M Z M L Y G K S T T R N W K Q S D
N S V B F P H L K S J L B M D L G Y S Y Q X G R
D K Q V L T S K Z C M Y M T L B T V S B R X F J
```

Word Box

swim	climb	jog	build	laugh
run	read	throw	break	smile
jump	sleep	catch	eat	frown
skip	play	look	paint	cry
hop	slide	listen	yawn	cough

Name _____

Words

Find the word "word" twenty times in the word search puzzle. It can be found across, down, or diagonally.

```
W O R D Z Y T Z W O R D Q Z B W S V Q W V M H P
M T X R S R F X C Q G P L R T W O R D N Z V X T
G T S X S V C C W L T G M W H L B Q X T W O R D
K Y B G Q C V C M O K R H O T V M G J K N K C G
J V V P W W K Y T Y R J M R K D M R V K S N R W
D K V P D O V P F Q F D R D V T G R D H H P L O
Y T S J R R R V Z R Y P C Z G Y T R W W O R D R
D Z W Y H D N G W Y W O R D B G O F T R G D G D
J Z O W P N W B F O L F F Y L W M G R D H J T J
W O R D D M V T J T R L L Y F P Y X S V W X X H
T C D X F Y X J S R M D Q Z V C D Z Y C O P W G
H T R D N G N Y R W B P V P C Z V Y W F R M M D
T P W W Q F K K D O F J P N F M D C N H D J K S
X B L C W D D Q S R M S J T R R B V Y M T W V C
T D Y J S K K K Z D G R B F O Z X V C F F O V N
B V R S W Y C D T Q Y N G W N V W G D Z G R X R
M B B P D W O R D V B D M N R C F Q W O R D S H
T F U P K V G B M F W R T F U P K V G B M F W R
V Z R P K T F D V J Y L V Z R P K T F D V J Y L
L K V T F R E S C V H U L K V T F R E S C V H U
J C L P S C Z X M N Y B J C L P S C Z X M N Y B
K G D S A V T H J A V I K G D S A V T H J A V I
```

Name _____

Scrambled Words

Unscramble the letters to find the barnyard animals.

1. neh _____

2. gip _____

3. rhsoe _____

4. owc _____

5. osgeo _____

6. kdcu _____

7. srotore _____

8. lume _____

9. gato _____

10. tca _____

11. hpsee _____

12. gdo _____

Name _____

More Scrambled Words

Unscramble the letters to find the musical instruments.

1. rmsdu _____

2. lutef _____

3. utrgia _____

4. opani _____

5. joanb _____

6. olinvi _____

7. buta _____

8. angtrlie _____

9. arhp _____

10. booe _____

11. lceol _____

12. goran _____

16

Name _____

Word Jumbles

Unscramble the letters to find the things used in a house.

1. dbe _____

2. mlpa _____

3. voen _____

4. lvsnteeiio _____

5. batle _____

6. nkis _____

7. salgs _____

8. hraic _____

9. lewto _____

10. lptea _____

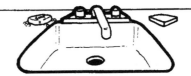

11. ubt _____

12. rkfo _____

Name _____

Decoding

Match each number to the letter in the code to find the color names.

A	B	C	D	E	F	G	H	I	J	K	L	M
1	2	3	4	5	6	7	8	9	10	11	12	13

N	O	P	Q	R	S	T	U	V	W	X	Y	Z
14	15	16	17	18	19	20	21	22	23	24	25	26

1. 2 12 21 5 _____

2. 18 5 4 _____

3. 16 21 18 16 12 5 _____

4. 7 18 5 5 14 _____

5. 2 12 1 3 11 _____

6. 25 5 12 12 15 23 _____

7. 23 8 9 20 5 _____

8. 19 9 12 22 5 18 _____

9. 15 18 1 14 7 5 _____

10. 16 9 14 11 _____

11. 7 15 12 4 _____

12. 2 18 15 23 14 _____

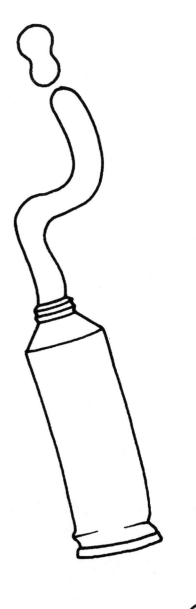

Name _____

Word Codes

To decode the words below, write the letter of the alphabet that comes after each letter given. The words you spell will be things found at school. (**Note:** Use "Z" as the letter before "A.")

1. odmbhk   _____

2. bgzkj   _____

3. rstcdms   _____

4. fknad   _____

5. okzxfqntmc   _____

6. sdzbgdq   _____

7. cdrj   _____

8. dqzrdq   _____

9. bqzxnmr   _____

10. ozodq   _____

11. oqhmbhozk   _____

12. qtkdq   _____

Name _____

What Comes Next?

Draw the next thing in each series.

1.

2.

3.

4.

5.

Name _____

Number Series

Write the next number in each series.

1. 1 2 3 1 2 3 1 2   _____

2. 1 2 2 1 2 2 1 2   _____

3. 1 2 1 2 1 2 1 2   _____

4. 1 1 1 2 2 2 3 3   _____

5. 1 2 3 4 1 2 3 4   _____

6. 1 2 3 2 1 2 3 2   _____

7. 1 2 2 3 3 3 4 4 4   _____

8. 1 1 2 2 1 1 3 3 1   _____

9. 1 1 2 1 1 3 1 1 2   _____

10. 1 5 1 10 1 15 1 20 1   _____

11. 10 9 8 7 6 5 4 3 2   _____

12. 1 2 4 8 16 32   _____

Name _____

Letter Series

Write the next letter in each series.

1. A B C D E F G H I J _____

2. L M N O P Q R S T U _____

3. Z Y X W V U T S R Q _____

4. A A B B C C D D E E _____

5. A B A C A D A E A F _____

6. A B B C C C D D D _____

7. A B C X Y Z A B C X _____

8. A A A B C C C D E E _____

9. A E I O U A E I O U _____

10. A A A B B B C C C D _____

11. A Z Z Z A Z Z Z A Z Z A _____

12. A B C B A B C B A B _____

Name _____

Alphabet Train

Fill in the missing uppercase letters of the alphabet.

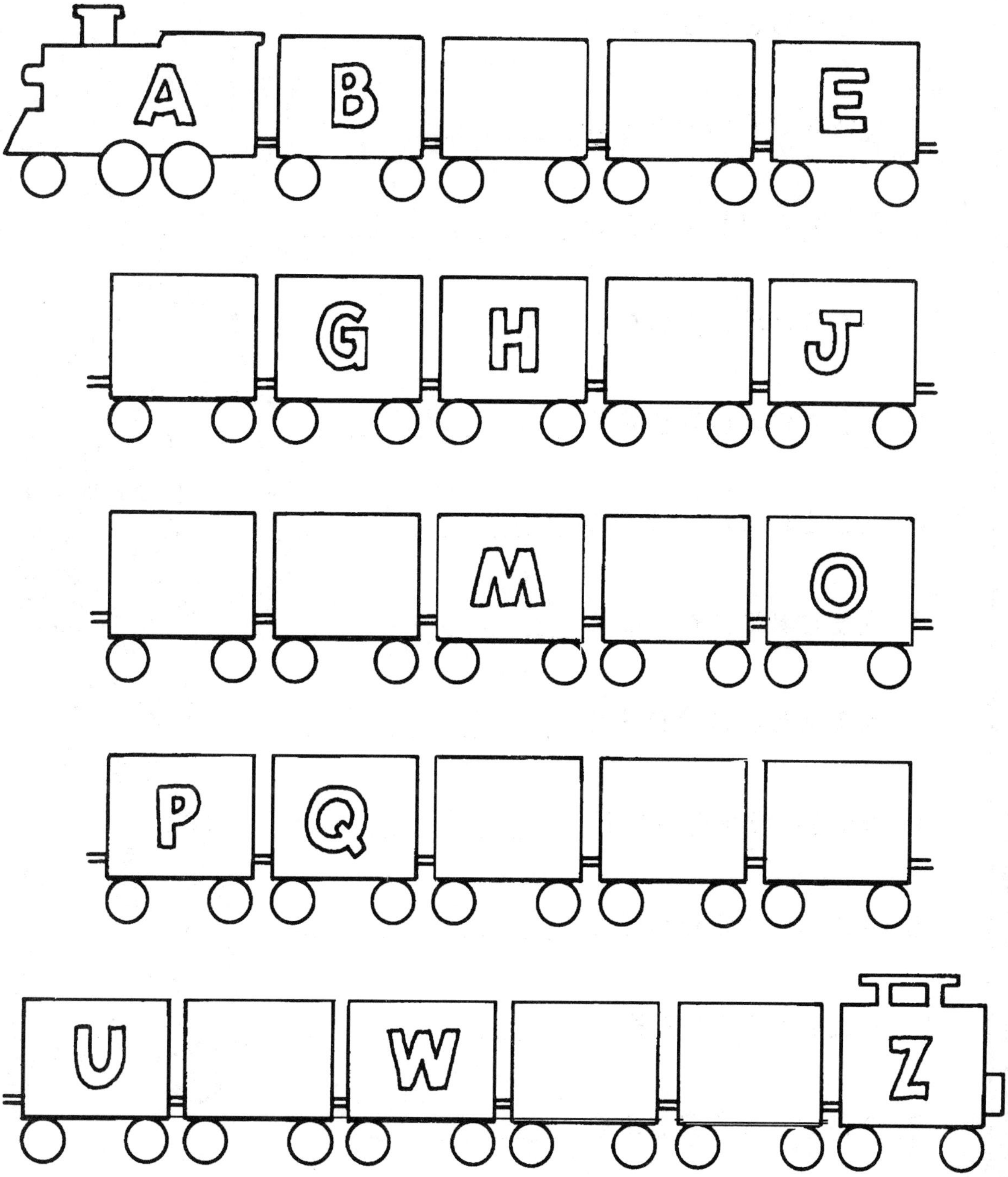

A B □ □ E

□ G H □ J

□ □ M □ O

P Q □ □ □

U □ W □ □ Z

Name _____

Alpha-Bug

Fill in the missing lowercase letters of the alphabet.

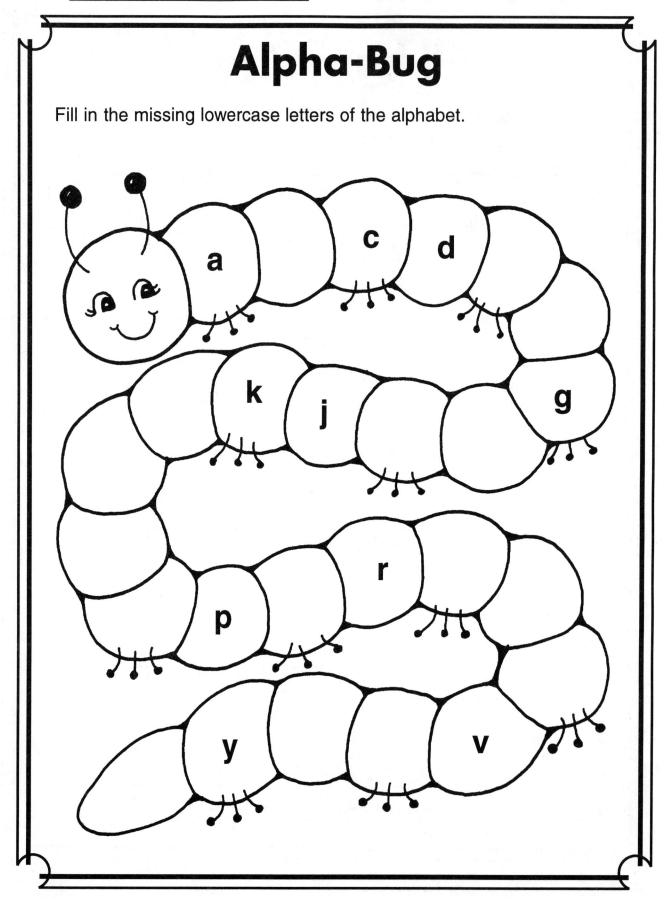

Name _____

Alphabetical Order

Put the words in alphabetical order.

mirror	baby
football	monkey
bath	dress
igloo	wombat
wooly	ice
dash	foot

1._____

2._____

3._____

4._____

5._____

6._____

7._____

8._____

9._____

10._____

11._____

12._____

Name _____

More Alphabetical Order

Put the words in alphabetical order.

play	zipper
zoo	lazy
bring	coyote
leopard	playground
camp	lamp
brought	pickle

1._____

2._____

3._____

4._____

5._____

6._____

7._____

8._____

9._____

10._____

11._____

12._____

Name _____

Lowercase

Write the lowercase letter for each uppercase letter.

A____   B____   C____   D____

E____   F____   G ____   H____

I____   J____   K____   L____

M____   N____   O____   P____

Q____   R____   S____   T____

U____   V____   W____   X____

Y____   Z____

Name _____

Uppercase

Write the uppercase letter for each lowercase letter.

a _____ b _____ c _____ d _____

e _____ f _____ g _____ h _____

i _____ j _____ k _____ l _____

m _____ n _____ o _____ p _____

q _____ r _____ s _____ t _____

u _____ v _____ w _____ x _____

y _____ z _____

Name _____

Ow

Color every box that has an "ow" in its spelling.

flower	pouring	frown
door	cow	horn
clown	four	crow
tower	gown	floor

Name _____

Br

Color every box that begins with "br."

Name _____

Sh

Color every box that begins with "sh."

Name _____

Silent Letters

Color every box that has a silent letter in its spelling.

wagon	cane	comb
horse	light bulb	moon
lamp	lamb	truck
goose	fish	five

32

Name _____

Beginning Letters

Write the letter that begins each word. Color the pictures.

letter _____   letter _____   letter _____

letter _____   letter _____   letter _____

letter _____   letter _____   letter _____

letter _____   letter _____   letter _____

Name _____

More Beginning Letters

Write the letter that begins each word. Color the pictures.

letter _____   letter _____   letter _____

letter _____   letter _____   letter _____

letter _____   letter _____   letter _____

letter _____   letter _____   letter _____

Name _____

Pairs

Color the item in each row that makes a pair with the first item.

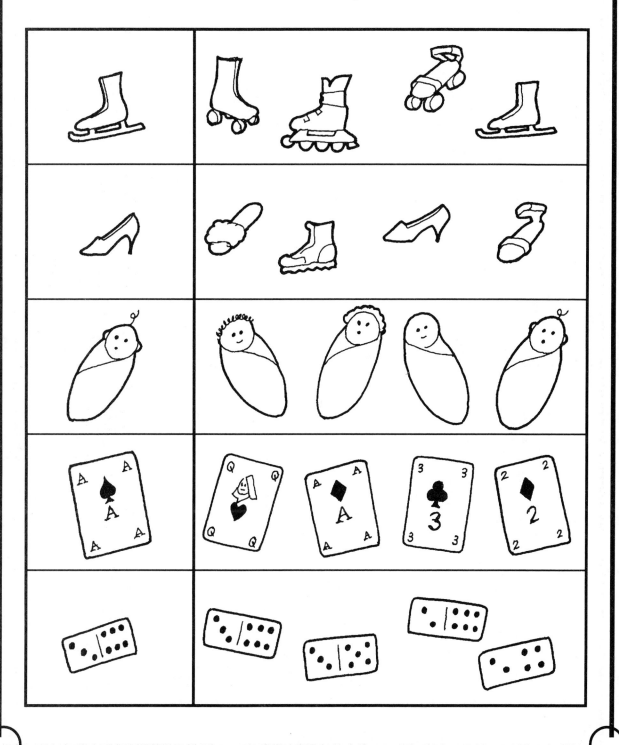

Name _____

Make a Set

Match the things that go together. Color the pictures.

Name _____

What Goes Together?

Match the things that go together. Color the pictures.

Name _____

"Mirror, Mirror, on the Wall"

Match the fairy tale figures that go together. Color the pictures.

Name _____

Hooves and Paws

Match the animal faces and feet. Color the pictures.

1.

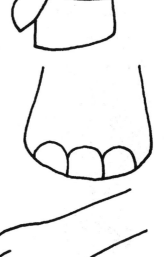

A.

2.

B.

3.

C.

4.

D.

5.

E.

39   *#486 Brain Teasers — Grade 1*

Name _____

It Doesn't Belong

Circle everything in the picture that does not belong. Color the picture.

Name _____

Two by Two

Color everything that comes in twos.

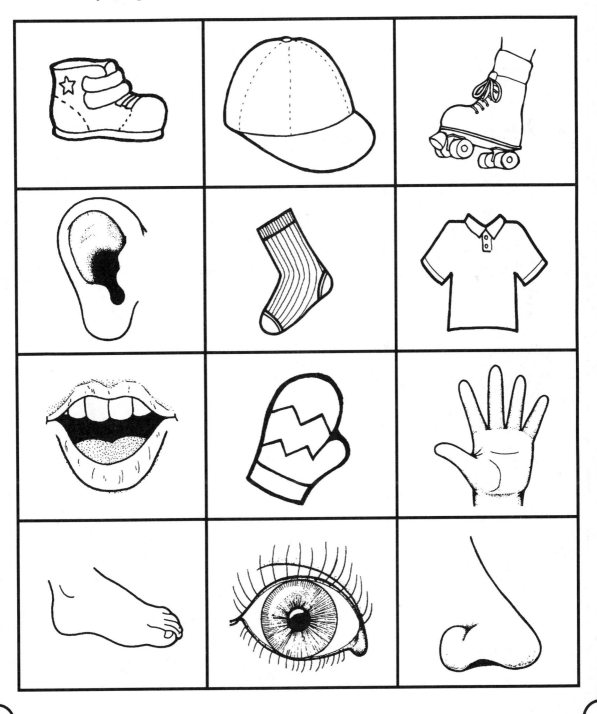

Name _____

What Do We Wear?

Color everything that a person might wear.

Name _____

Whose Baby?

Which baby goes to which parent? Find the things in common, and you will know.

A.

Baby #_____

B.

Baby #_____

C.

Baby #_____

D.

Baby #_____

1

2

3

4

Name _____

Whose Is It?

Can you use the clues in the pictures to figure out what item belongs to each child? **Hint:** Think of the *number* of things. Write what each child owns on the line under his or her picture.

Mindy owns a _____ .   Pam owns a _____ .

Simon owns a _____ .

tricycle   bicycle

skateboard

Name _____

A Present for Everyone

Can you match each present to each child? **Hint:** The ones that go together have something in common. Write the present on the line under each child.

 Dawn

 Bill

 Emily

 Sue

Ken

bicycle

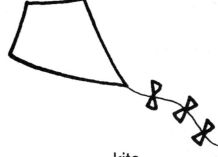

kite

doll

earrings

skates

Name _____

Package Math

Complete the problem on each package. The answer will be a clue to the present inside. Write the present on the line under each package.

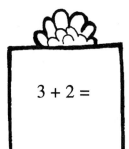 3 + 2 =

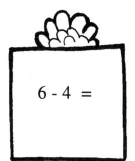 6 - 4 =

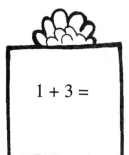 1 + 3 =

_____   _____   _____

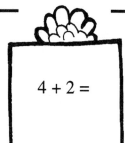 4 + 2 =

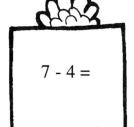 7 - 4 =

_____   _____

Cars

Bears

Dominoes

Dolls

Books

Name _____

More Package Math

Complete the problem on each package. The answer will be a clue to the present inside. Write the present on the line under each package.

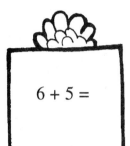

$6 + 5 =$

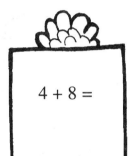

$4 + 8 =$

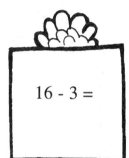

$16 - 3 =$

_____ _____ _____

$15 - 5 =$

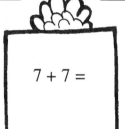

$7 + 7 =$

_____ _____

Marbles

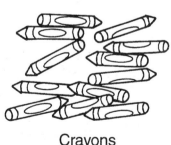

Crayons

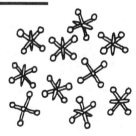

Jacks

Tops

Paintbrushes

Name _____

Favorite Sports

Three friends, Tran, Henry, and Maya, each enjoy a different sport. When they play together, they take turns choosing the game they will play. Use the clues below to figure out each child's favorite sport. Draw a line to connect each child to his or her favorite sport.

1. Tran's favorite sport uses a bat.
2. Henry's favorite sport uses a hoop.
3. Maya's favorite sport does not use a bat or a hoop.

Tran

soccer

Henry

baseball

Maya

basketball

Name _____

How Old Are They?

There are three children, Susie, Jimmy, and Katie. They are each different ages. One child is 6, another is 7, and the third is 8-years-old. Can you use the clues below to figure out the age of each child? Draw a line to each child's correct age.

1. Susie is two years older than Jimmy.
2. Katie is in the middle.
3. Jimmy is the youngest.

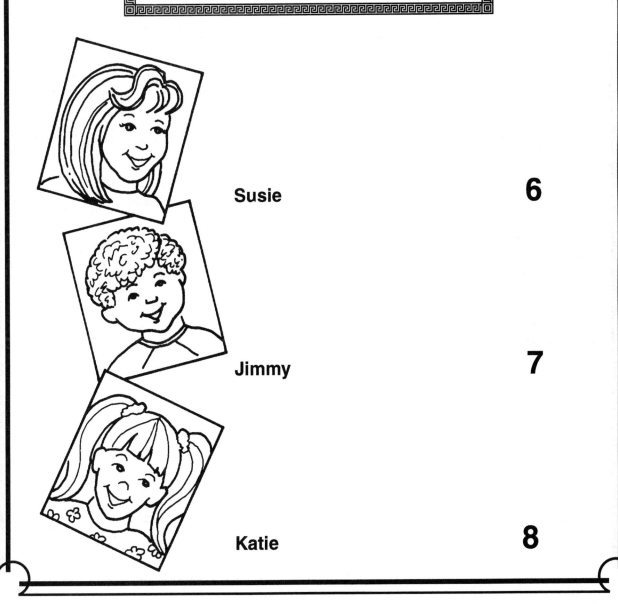

Susie   **6**

Jimmy   **7**

Katie   **8**

                   #486 Brain Teasers — Grade 1

Name _____

Which Is Different?

One picture in each row is different. Color the picture that is different.

Name _____

Whose Balloon?

Follow the strings to see who is connected to which balloon. Write the number of the balloon below each child. Color the pictures.

Balloon # ____ **Balloon #** ____ **Balloon #** ____ **Balloon #** ____ **Balloon #** ____

Name _____

Dog Day

What a tangle! Can you figure out which dog goes to which owner?
Write the number of each dog above each owner. Color the pictures.

Dog # _____   Dog # _____   Dog # _____   Dog # _____   Dog # _____

Name _____

How Many Circles?

How many circles are in the picture? Count them and then color the picture.

There are _____ circles.

Name _____

How Many Squares?

How many squares are in the picture? Count them and then color the picture.

There are _____ squares.

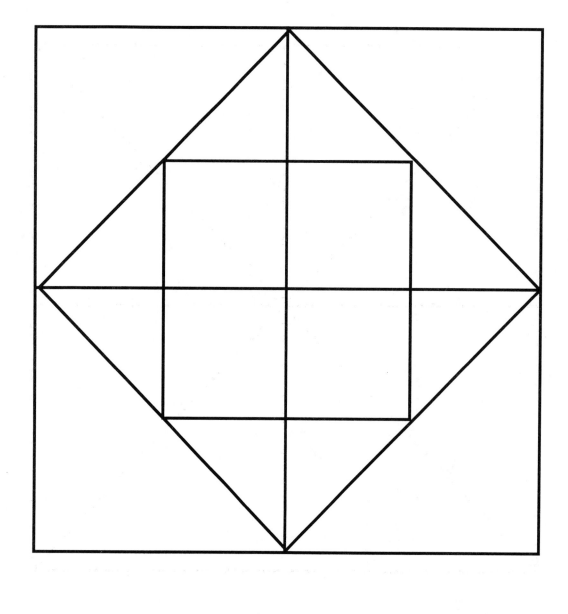

Name _____

How Many Triangles?

How many triangles are in the picture? Count them and then color
the picture.

There are _____ triangles.

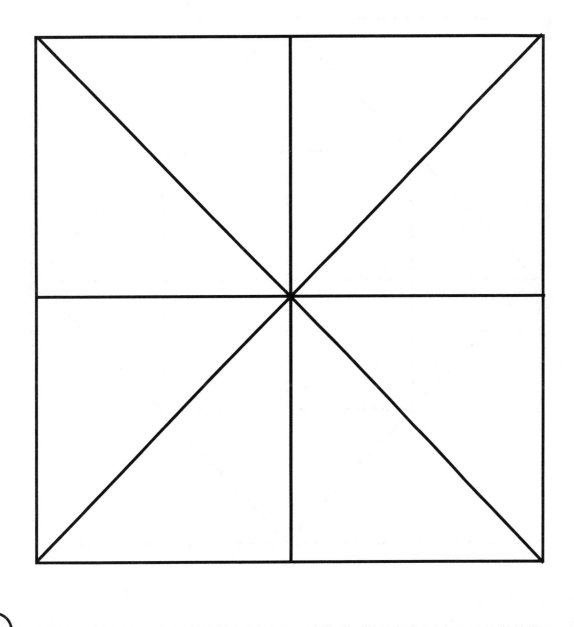

Name _____

Football

Answer the questions. Color the picture.

1. How many footballs are there? _____

2. How many legs are there? _____

3. How many players are there? _____

4. How many shoes are there? _____

5. What else can you count? _____

Name _____

Outer Space

Answer the questions. Color the picture.

1. How many planets are there? _____

2. How many stars are there? _____

3. How many space ships are there? _____

4. How many rings around planets are there? _____

5. What else can you count? _____

Name _____

Ballet

Answer the questions. Color the picture.

1. How many people are there? _____

2. How many tutus are there? _____

3. How many roses are there? _____

4. How many ballet slippers are there? _____

5. What else can you count? _____

Name _____

Sets of Five

Color every set of five items.

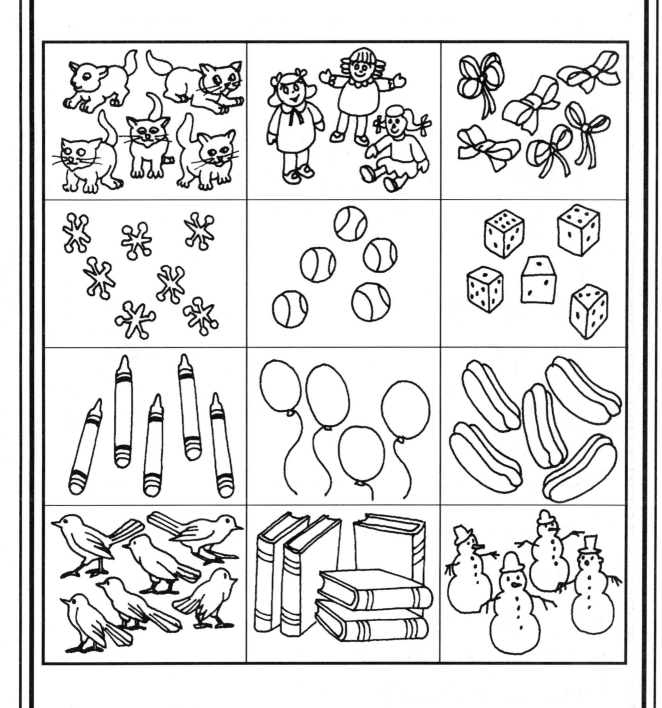

Name _____

Sets of Ten

Complete each set to make a set of ten items. Color the pictures.

60

Name _____

Find the Dozen

Look at the picture below. Find the animal that comes in a set of twelve. Then, color the picture.

There are 12 _____ .

Fill in the Blanks

Name _____

Missing Word

What word is missing from each set of words?

1. _____ Bo Peep

   _____ Boy Blue

   _____ Red Riding Hood

2. The _____ Little Pigs

   The _____ Bears

   The _____ Billy Goats Gruff

3. Rockabye _____

   Bye Bye _____ Bunting

   Hush, Little _____

4. _____ Mother Hubbard

   This _____ Man

   The _____ Woman in the Shoe

Name _____

Missing Letters

Fill in the missing letter to complete each word.

1. co___d

2. hap___y

3. fun___y

4. c___w

5. cro___

6. mo___her

7. rabbi___

8. jac___et

9. m___uth

10. ___ise

11. s___reet

12. ho___se

13. monke___

14. ___lamp

15. pock___t

Name _____

More Missing Letters

Fill in the missing letter to complete each word.

1. s__ring

2. bac__

3. __ix

4. hai__

5. poli__e

6. e__bow

7. s__eet

8. stomac__

9. flo__r

10. co__ch

11. __lanket

12. __cout

13. chan__e

14. fin__er

15. p__ease

Name _____

What's Missing?

Draw in the missing part of each picture.

bird

cat

zebra

dog

kangaroo

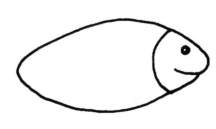

fish

Name _____

Complete the Picture

Draw in the missing part of each picture.

face

slide

clock

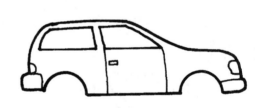

car

sailboat

umbrella

Name _____

Mother Goose

Fill in the missing words in the Mother Goose rhymes.

1. Jack be _____ ,

   Jack be _____ ,

   Jack _____ over the candlestick.

2. Mary, Mary, quite _____

   How does your _____ grow?

3. Diddle, diddle, dumpling, my _____ John

   Went to _____ with his trousers on.

4. Jack and _____

   Went up the _____

   To fetch a _____ of water.

   Jack _____ down

   And _____ his crown,

   And Jill came _____ after.

5. Little Miss Muffet _____ on her tuffet

   _____ her curds and whey.

   Along came a _____ who sat down beside her

   And frightened Miss Muffet _____ .

Name _____

Fairy Tales

Fill in the missing words from the fairy tale titles.

1. The Three Little _____

2. Goldilocks and the Three _____

3. The Three _____ Goats Gruff

4. _____ White and the _____ Dwarfs

5. The _____ Mermaid

6. Beauty and the _____

7. Aladdin and the Magic _____

8. _____ and the Beanstalk

9. The _____ That Laid the Golden _____

10. The Bremen _____ Musicians

11. _____ Beauty

12. The _____ Princess

13. The Steadfast _____ Soldier

14. The Tale of Peter _____

Name _____

Rhymes

Write four words that rhyme with each word below.

ten

_____

_____

_____

_____

bee

_____

_____

_____

_____

do

_____

_____

_____

_____

top

_____

_____

_____

_____

bat

_____

_____

_____

_____

peep

_____

_____

_____

_____

Name _____

Opposites

List the opposites.

1. hot _____

2. dark _____

3. off _____

4. over _____

5. high _____

6. in _____

7. far _____

8. curly _____

9. up _____

10. empty _____

11. happy _____

12. wet _____

13. soft _____

14. tall _____

15. clean _____

Name _____

Days of the Week

Write the day that falls between the two days given.

1. Sunday   _____ Tuesday

2. Thursday   _____ Saturday

3. Monday   _____ Wednesday

4. Friday   _____ Sunday

5. Wednesday _____ Friday

6. Tuesday   _____ Thursday

7. Saturday   _____ Monday

Name _____

Months of the Year

Write the month that falls between the two months given.

1. January   _____ March

2. June   _____ August

3. October   _____ December

4. February   _____ April

5. July   _____ September

6. September _____ November

7. March   _____ May

8. August   _____ October

9. April   _____ June

10. November _____ January

11. May   _____ July

12. December _____ February

Name _____

Name Something

1. Name something red. _____

2. Name something tall. _____

3. Name something round. _____

4. Name something thin. _____

5. Name something fast. _____

6. Name something loud. _____

7. Name something blue. _____

8. Name something small. _____

9. Name something heavy. _____

10. Name something quiet. _____

11. Name something beautiful. _____

12. Name something large. _____

13. Name something hot. _____

14. Name something cold. _____

15. Name something happy. _____

Name _____

Sand Castle

Who lives in this sand castle? Draw a picture to show who it is.

74

Name _____

Shoes

Who wears these shoes? Draw a picture to show who it is.

Answer Key

Page 3
giraffe

Page 4
castle

Page 5
whale

Page 6
schoolhouse

Page 7

Page 8

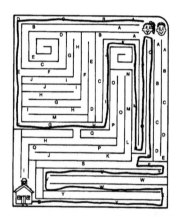

Page 9

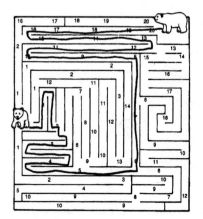

Page 10

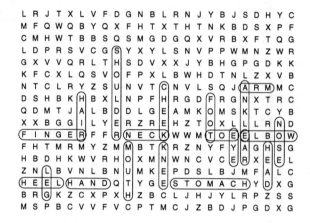

Page 11

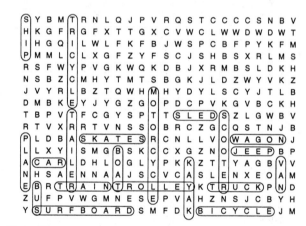

Page 12

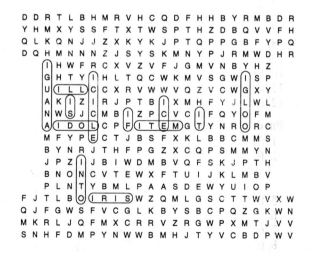

</>
Page 13

```
N R N B S W S P M R N J N L R L B S H K M J R Z
X R N L G V S C P L G W N P A G I U F Q R H J K
S R M X J H B V C N G F D L R U R S E Y U U
M L B T L D N Z V A L F H A E U G X T L A G M S
S L O O K F P A I N T C R Y A W N H J E D Q P X
K W Y R V Q S Q P T H C F O T M T R O E N X R M
I B I V L N L N X N R B H C W L Z L G P H C K J
P W R M H Q I D P V O R X O P N T D L S F W V H
C S G E X P D F F K W D H U X J H D M Z N D F
L J K K A N E R N F B Y N G W F K O H I T Y T Q
I B Q T C K X Y Y D M C Y H X M H W P L Z W S B
M P N M M D Y R X G S L M Q T B X G L E D Y G C
B H W G V D C R V S V C Y G Z Z B Y H T X G S H
T V D W V W C P V W R F N P Y K Y M F T H Y V F
Q J V D R L F M Z M L Y G K S T T R N W K Q S D
N S V B F P H L K S J L B M D L G Y S Y Q X G R
D K Q V L T S K Z C M Y M T L B T V S B R X F J
```

Page 14

```
W O R D Z Y T Z W O R D Q Z B W S V Q W V M H P
M T X R S R F X C Q G P L R T W O R D N Z V X T
G T S X S V C C W L T G M W H L B Q X T W O R D
K Y B G Q C V C K R H O T V M G J K N K C G
J V V P W K Y T Y R J M R K D M R V K S N R W
D K V P D O Y F Q F D R D V T G R D R V K S N R
Y T S J R R V Z R Y P C Z G Y T R W O R D R
D Z W Y H D N G W Y W O R D B G O F T R G D G D
J Z O W P N W B F O L F F Y L W M G R D H J T J
W O R D D M V T J T R L L Y F P Y X S V W X X H
T C D X F Y X J S R M D Q Z V C D Z Y C O P W G
H T R D N G N Y R W B P V P N F M D C N H D J K S
T P W W Q F K K O F J P N F M M D C N H D J K S
X B L C W D D Q S R M S J T R B V Y M T W V C
T D Y J S K K K Z D G R B F O Z X V C F F O V W
B V R S W Y C D T Q Y N G W N V W G D Z G R X R
M B B P D W O R D V B D M N R C F Q W O R D S H
T F U P K V G B M F W R T F U P K V G B M F W R
V Z R P K T F D V J Y L V Z R P K T F D V J Y L
L K V T F R E S C V H U L K V T F R E S C V H U
J C L P S C Z X M N Y B J C L P S C Z X M N Y B
K G D S A V T H J A V I K G D S A V T H J A V I
```

Page 15

1. hen
2. pig
3. horse
4. cow
5. goose
6. duck
7. rooster
8. mule
9. goat
10. cat
11. sheep
12. dog

Page 16

1. drums
2. flute
3. guitar
4. piano
5. banjo
6. violin
7. tuba
8. triangle
9. harp
10. oboe
11. cello
12. organ

Page 17

1. bed
2. lamp
3. oven
4. television
5. table
6. sink
7. glass
8. chair
9. towel
10. plate
11. tub
12. fork

Page 18

1. blue
2. red
3. purple
4. green
5. black
6. yellow
7. white
8. silver
9. orange
10. pink
11. gold
12. brown

Page 19

1. pencil
2. chalk
3. student
4. globe
5. playground
6. teacher
7. desk
8. eraser
9. crayons
10. paper
11. principal
12. ruler

Page 20

1. heart
2. triangle
3. heart
4. triangle
5. square

Page 21

1. 3
2. 2
3. 1
4. 3
5. 1
6. 1
7. 4
8. 1
9. 1
10. 25
11. 1
12. 64

Page 22

1. K
2. V
3. P
4. F
5. A
6. E
7. Y
8. E
9. A
10. D
11. Z
12. C

Page 23

C D F I K L N R S T V X Y

Page 24

b e f h i l m n o q s t u w x z

Page 25

1. baby
2. bath
3. dash
4. dress
5. foot
6. football
7. ice
8. igloo
9. mirror
10. monkey
11. wombat
12. wooly

Page 26

1. bring
2. brought
3. camp
4. coyote
5. lamp
6. lazy
7. leopard
8. pickle
9. play
10. playground
11. zipper
12. zoo

Page 27

Aa Bb Cc Dd Ee Ff Gg Hh Ii Jj Kk Ll Mm Nn Oo Pp Qq Rr Ss Tt Uu Vv Ww Xx Yy Zz

Page 28

aA bB cC dD eE fF gG hH iI jJ kK lL mM nN oO pP qQ rR sS tT uU vV wW xX yY zZ

Page 29

flower, frown, cow, clown, crow, tower, gown

Page 30

brush, bride, bread, bridge, broken

Page 31

sheep, shop, shingle, shoe, shave, shawl

Page 32

cane, comb, horse, light bulb, lamb, goose, five

Page 33

H = hamburger
T = tricycle
N = necklace
C = circle
P = purse
E = eye
Q = queen
K = kite
S = skate
D = door
A = apple
B = bell

Page 34

U = umbrella
W = wheel
M = mouse
C = church
F = fan
I = igloo
L = lion
O = ostrich
Y = yo-yo
G = gate
R = ring
S = ship or B = boat

Page 35

ice skate, high-heeled shoe, one-curl baby, ace, matching domino

Page 36

fork and spoon, baseball and bat, baby and rattle, bird and nest, paper and pencil, and shoe and sock

Page 37

house and chimney, rubber duck and bathtub, tree and leaf, computer and disc, school and desk, and child and ball

Page 38

pumpkin and glass slipper, wolf and basket of goodies, bear and porridge, pig and straw house, and witch and apple

Page 39

1. C
2. D
3. E
4. B
5. A

Page 40

Circled: sailboat on the grass, hippo, fish in the sky, dog in the tree, television set, and giraffe

Page 41

shoe, skate, ear, sock, mitten, hand, foot, and eye

Page 42

jacket, shoe, hat, tie, sock, scarf

Page 43
A. 3
B. 4
C. 1
D. 2

Page 44
Mindy owns a bicycle.
Simon owns a tricycle.
Pam owns a skateboard.

Page 45
Dawn = doll
Bill = bicycle
Emily = earrings
Sue = skates
Ken = kite

Page 46
3 + 2 = 5 (bears)
6 - 4 = 2 (cars)
1 + 3 = 4 (dominoes)
4 + 2 = 6 (books)
7 - 4 = 3 (dolls)

Page 47
6 + 5 = 11 (tops)
4 + 8 = 12 (crayons)
16 - 3 = 13 (paintbrushes)
15 - 5 = 10 (jacks)
7 + 7 = 14 (marbles)

Page 48
Tran likes baseball.
Henry likes basketball.
Maya likes soccer.

Page 49
Susie is 8.
Jimmy is 6.
Katie is 7.

Page 50
Different picture: third, second, first, fourth, and second

Page 51
A. 4
B. 5
C. 2
D. 3
E. 1

Page 52
A. 4
B. 5
C. 1
D. 2
E. 3

Page 53
There are 9 circles.

Page 54
There are 11 squares.

Page 55
There are 16 triangles.

Page 56
1. 2
2. 15
3. 8
4. 13
5. Answers will vary depending on individual examination, perception, and creativity.

Page 57
1. 7
2. 13
3. 3
4. 6
5. Answers will vary depending on individual examination, perception, and creativity.

Page 58
1. 9
2. 4
3. 7
4. 15
5. Answers will vary depending on individual examination, perception, and creativity.

Page 59
kittens, balls, dice, crayons, hot dogs, and books

Page 60
3 more birds, 4 more candles, 1 more Valentine, and 5 more hats

Page 61
There are 12 rabbits.

Page 62
1. Little
2. Three
3. Baby
4. Old

Page 63
1. cold (l)
2. happy (p)
3. funny (n)
4. cow (o)
5. crow or crop (w or p)
6. mother (t)
7. rabbit (t)
8. jacket (k)
9. mouth (o)
10. rise or wise (r or w)
11. street (t)
12. horse or house (r or u)
13. monkey (y)
14. clamp (c)
15. pocket (e)

Page 64
1. spring or string (p or t)
2. back (k)
3. six, mix, or fix (s, m, or f)
4. hair or hail (r of l)
5. polite or police (t or c)
6. elbow (l)
7. sheet, sleet, or sweet (h, l, or w)
8. stomach (h)
9. floor or flour (o or u)
10. coach or couch (a or u)
11. blanket (b)
12. scout (s)
13. change or chance (g or c)
14. finger (g)
15. please (l)

Page 65
the bird's beak, the cat's tail, the zebra's stripes, the dog's ears, the kangaroo's pouch, and the fish's fins

Page 66
the face's nose, the slide's ladder, the clock's hands, the car's wheels, the sailboat's sail, and the umbrella's handle

Page 67
1. nimble, quick, jump
2. contrary, garden
3. son, bed
4. Jill, hill, pail, fell, broke, tumbling
5. sat, eating, spider, away

Page 68
1. Pigs
2. Bears
3. Billy
4. Snow, Seven
5. Little
6. Beast
7. Lamp
8. Jack
9. Goose, Eggs
10. Town
11. Sleeping
12. Swan
13. Tin
14. Rabbit

Page 69
Answers will vary.

Page 70
1. cold
2. light
3. on
4. under
5. low
6. out
7. near
8. straight
9. down
10. full
11. sad
12. dry
13. hard
14. short
15. dirty

Page 71
1. Monday
2. Friday
3. Tuesday
4. Saturday
5. Thursday
6. Wednesday
7. Sunday

Page 72
1. February
2. July
3. November
4. March
5. August
6. October
7. April
8. September
9. May
10. December
11. June
12. January

Page 73
Answers will vary.

Page 74
Picture responses will vary.

Page 75
Picture responses will vary.